Delicious Indian Snacks

15 delicious and easy to prepare Indian "street food" recipes

By M. Fredrick

Copyright © 2017

All Rights Reserved

Introduction

India is known for a lot of things, however one of the key elements of experiencing India is tasting Indian food. Especially the street food.

India is a nation of such cultural diversity that almost every city has its own specialty when it comes to food. The country's wide varieties of delicious (and cheap) street foods are known to be of great demand with locals and travellers alike.

In this book, I have compiled a list of 15 delicious and easy to prepare Indian street food recipes that I'm sure you will enjoy. Also, *towards the end of this book there are 3 bonus chutney recipes (coz Indians love their chutney) that are super easy to prepare and can be made in under 15 mins.*

Thank you for downloading this book and hope you enjoy reading it. I also hope you have just as much fun preparing and trying out the recipes as I had putting them together for you.

TABLE OF CONTENTS

1) Introduction
2) Falooda, Delicious Dessert Beverage
3) Crispy Aloo Pakoras (Potato Fritters)
4) Crispy Aloo Tikki (Potato Patty)
5) Mixed Vegetable Pakoras
6) Khaman (Besan) Dhokla
7) Masala Vada (Vadai)
8) Aloo Chana Chaat
9) Jhaal Muri – Kolkata Puffed Rice Snack
10) Aloo Chaat (Spicy Potato Snack)
11) Kulcha (Punjabi Flatbread)
12) Aloo Tikki (Potato Patties)
13) Dabeli Spicy Potato Sandwich
14) Batata Vada – Aloo Bonda (Fried Potato Dumpling)
15) Kulfi (Indian Eggless Ice Cream)
16) Vegetable Frankie – Kathi Roll

CHUTNEY

1) Hari Chutney – Cilantro Chutney
2) Tamarind Chutney
3) Coconut Chutney

A NOTE OF THANKS

Falooda, Delicious Dessert Beverage

Course: Dessert

Prep Time 5 minutes

Cook Time 20 minutes

Total Time 25 minutes

Servings 4 people

Ingredients

- 2-1/2 Cup milk
- 3 Tbsp sugar (divided)
- 1 Cup fresh mango pulp
- 2 Tbsp sweet basil seed (tukmaria, sabza)
- 1 oz packet of falooda (falooda is a corn vermicelli)
- 6 scoops vanilla ice-cream
- 1/2 cup finely chopped mangos (for garnishing)

Method

1. Boil the milk with 2 tablespoons of sugar for about 15 minutes after milk comes to boil or until till it reduces to about 1-1/2 cup. After milk cool off refrigerate, milk should be chill.

2. Cook the falooda in boiling water, till they are soft! Strain, and chopped them in few pieces and keep aside to cool. Then refrigerator till needed, and it is chilled.

3. Add about 2 table spoons of sugar to mango pulp or as needed depends on sweetness of mango. Refrigerate the mango pulp and chopped mango, till you are ready to use.

4. Soak the basil seeds/ tukmaria in a bowl in about ¼ cup of water making sure seeds are completely submerge. They will soon start to swell and look transparent. Strain and keep aside in a small bowl.

5. Milk and falooda should be refrigerated till you are ready to use, you can prepare them in advance as they can be refrigerated for 3-4 days.

6. Time to assemble the falooda, it is layered beverage-desert, take a tall glass first put 2-3 tablespoons of mango pulp, few spoons of falooda, about 2 spoons of baisel seeds, pour about ¼ cup of milk, about 1or 2 scoops of ice-cream, again some falooda and garnish with chopped mango.

Crispy Aloo Pakoras (Potato Fritters)

This recipe will serve 4.

Ingredients

- 2 cups potatoes wash, peeled and finely chopped
- 1/2 cup besan
- 2 tablespoons rice flour
- 2 tablespoons corn starch
- 1 tablespoon fennel seeds crushed, saunf
- 1 tablespoon coriander seed crushed, dhania
- 1/4 teaspoon turmeric, haldi
- 1/4 teaspoon mango powder, amchoor
- 1/8 teaspoon asafetida, hing
- 1-1/2 teaspoons red chili flakes
- 1 tablespoon ginger finely chopped, adrak
- 2 tablespoons cilantro chopped, hara dhania
- 1 tablespoon oil
- 1 teaspoon salt

Also need oil to fry

Method

1. Wash and peel the potatoes and cut them in very small cubes, and soak them in cold water.

2. Mix all the ingredients together except salt and potatoes.

3. Drain the water from potatoes, add the spice mix and mix it well. Add water as needed making sure the spice mix stick to the potatoes uniformly.

4. Now add the salt and mix it well.

5. Heat the oil in a frying pan on medium high heat.

6. The frying pan should have at least 1 inch of oil. To check if the oil is ready, put one piece of potato in the oil. The potato should raise to the top but not change color right away.

7. While putting the potatoes into oil, loosen them with your fingers to make sure the potatoes are separated and do not form clutter. Potatoes should be separated while frying.

8. Fry the potatoes until they turn light brown, turning them occasionally.

9. When they are done cooking, take them out of the oil with a slotted spoon. Place them on a paper towel to absorb the extra oil.

Crispy aloo pakoras taste best when they are served hot. Serve the with cilantro chutney and hot cup of masala chai.

Crispy Aloo Tikki (Potato Patty)

This recipe will make 8 tikkies.

Ingredients:

For aloo tikki

- 4 cups potatoes boiled peeled and shredded
- 2 tablespoons corn starch
- 1 teaspoon salt
- 2 tablespoons cilantro finely chopped (hara dhania)
- Also need oil to shallow fry

For Chola Topping

- 1 15oz can of chick pea, garbanzo beans, kabuli chana,
- 2 tablespoons oil
- 2 tablespoons besan (gram flour)
- 2 tablespoons green chili finely chopped, adjust to taste
- 2 tablespoons ginger finely chopped, adjust to taste
- 1 teaspoon salt
- 1/2 teaspoon black salt
- 1 teaspoon roasted cumin seeds powder
- 1 teaspoon garam masala
- 1/2 teaspoon mango powder (amchoor)

Method

Preparation for potatoes

1. Boil the potatoes you will need 3 to 4 potatoes, do not overcook the potatoes they should be still firm, otherwise potatoes will be mushy, and tikki will not be crispy as desired. Peel and shred the potatoes.

2. Add salt, corn starch, and cilantro to shredded potatoes and mix it well with light hand. Don't knead the potatoes. Divide the potatoes in eight equal parts and roll them, into patties. Cover the patties and refrigerate for at least 4-5 hours. This step will make sure the tikkies are crispy.

Chola Topping

1. Wash the chick peas changing the water 2-3 times. In a blender mash the chick peas with one cup of water just churning few times. Chick peas should be mashed not pasty.

2. Heat the oil in a pan over medium heat add the besan and roast the besan stirring continuously until besan is golden brown this should take about a minute.

3. Add ginger and green chili stir for 30 seconds, add chick peas, salt, cumin seed powder, garam masala, and mango powder.

4. Cook over low heat for about 10 minutes if needed add water, chick peas should be consistency of dosa or pancake batter.

5. Turn off the heat,

Spiced chola topping should be served hot on top of the crispy aloo tikki.

Mixed Vegetable Pakoras

This Recipe will serve 6.

Ingredients:

- 1 cup potato peeled and cut into very small pieces
- 1 cup cauliflower cut into very small pieces
- 1 cup packed spinach roughly chopped
- 1 cup cabbage thinly sliced
- 2 green chilies finely chopped adjust to taste
- 1-1/2 cups besan (gram flour)
- 3 teaspoons oil
- 1 tablespoon coriander coarsely ground (Dhania)
- 1 tablespoon fennel seeds coarsely ground (saunf)
- 1/8 teaspoon asafetida
- 1/2 teaspoon red chili powder
- 1/2 teaspoon mango powder (amchoor)
- 1/4 teaspoon garam masala
- 1-1/2 teaspoons salt
- Oil to fry

Method

1. Combine all the dry ingredients, besan, coriander, fennel, red pepper, salt, and asafetida in a bowl. Mix it well.

2. Add potatoes, cauliflower, spinach, cabbage, and green chilies and oil into dry mix, mix it well keep aside for about ten minutes. When you are ready to fry pakoras if mix is too dry add as needed 1 or 2 spoons of water to make texture of soft dough.

3. Heat at least one inch of oil in a frying pan over medium high heat. To test, put one drop of batter in the oil. The batter should come up and not change color instantly.

4. Place about two tablespoons of mix holding with your fingers into the oil. Do not overlap the pakoras.

5. Fry the pakoras in small batches; after you turn the pakoras one time press the pakoras lightly.

6. This will take five to six minutes per batch. Fry the pakoras, turning occasionally, until both sides are golden brown.

7. Repeat this process for the remaining batches.

8. The crispy, delicious pakoras are now ready to serve.

Khaman (Besan) Dhokla

This recipe will serve 6.

Ingredients:

- 1-1/2 cups besan (Gram flour)
- 2 tablespoons Sooji (rava, Semolina)
- 1/2 teaspoon Citric acid
- 1/8 teaspoon asafetida (hing)
- 1/4 teaspoon turmeric (haldi)
- 3 teaspoons sugar
- 1 teaspoon ginger paste
- 1 green chili finely chopped
- 1 teaspoon salt
- 1-1/4 cups water use as needed to make pouring consistency
- 2-1/2 teaspoons Eno (fruit Salt)

For Seasoning:

- 2 tablespoons oil
- 1/2 teaspoon mustard seeds (rai)
- 1/2 teaspoon sesame seeds (til)
- 4-5 curry leaves optional
- 2 green chili seeded and cut into 4 length wise

Also need 2-3 tablespoons hot water

Utensils to steam Dhokla

Dhokla maker – or, if you don't have that, use all three of the following:

- Covered pan large enough to hold round cake rack
- Round cake-cooling rack

- Round 9" cake pan

Method

1. Sift the besan, and make batter should be smooth and pouring consistency. Add all the ingredients except the ENO (fruit salt) to the batter sooji, salt, sugar, asafetida, ginger, citric acid and green chili, mix it well, if needed add little more water. Set aside. We can add the ENO just before steaming.

2. Grease the cake pan and set aside.

3. Set the cake rack in the pan. Add water, just enough to touch the cake rack, and bring to a boil. This will be used to steam the dhokla.

4. When the water boils, turn down the heat to medium.

5. Add the ENO to the batter and beat the batter for a minute, batter will become airy and frothy. Quickly pour batter into a greased cake pan. Place the cake pan into the saucepan over the cake rack. Cover the pan. Steam for about 8 minutes on medium heat. Do not open the pan in between.

6. Check Dhokla with a knife. If the knife comes out clean, dhokla is ready. Turn off the heat and let it sit over the stem for 4-5 minutes covered.

Prepare the seasoning

1. Heat oil in a small pan over medium heat moderately. Add mustard seeds, and sesame seeds stir for 3-4 seconds, add green chili stir and curry leaves, stir for few seconds. Cover the pan and turn off the heat. Careful curry leaves will splatter.

2. First drizzle the hot water over dhokla this will keep the dhokla moist. Then drizzle the seasoning over.

3. Cut them in squares.

4. Serve with Hari cilantro chutney.

Taste best when it is served warm.

Masala Vada (Vadai)

Recipe will serve 6.

Ingredients:

- 1 cup chana dal or also known Bengal gram
- 1 tablespoons rice flour
- 1 cup potatoes boiled peeled and mashed
- 1 teaspoon salt
- 1-1/2 teaspoons fennel seeds crushed
- 1 teaspoon mango powder
- 1/2 teaspoon black pepper crushed
- 1/8 teaspoon asafetida
- 1 tablespoon ginger paste
- 2 tablespoons finely chopped green chilies
- 1/4 cup cilantro finely chopped

Also need oil to fry

Method

1. Wash and Soak chana dal in three cups of water for about 4 hours after soaking this will become about twice in volume.

2. Drain the water, keep 2 tablespoons soaked dal aside. Grind dal coarsely without adding any water. You can use the food processor.

3. Take out the dal in a mixing bowl, add all the ingredients, potatoes, rice flour, salt , fennel seeds, mango powder, black pepper, asafetida, ginger, green chili, cilantro and soaked chana dal. Mix it well.

4. Lightly wet your palms, this will make easy to roll the vadas. Take a lemon size ball of the mix, flatten it with your hands, making them to about half inch thick patties. This should make about 16 patties. Preferably make a few patties before starting to fry.

5. Heat the oil in a frying pan, (frying pan should have about 1" of oil) over medium heat. Oil should be moderately hot when you drop the vada, oil should sizzle and come to surface slowly. Gently drop the vadas in oil making sure they don't overlap.

6. Fry the vadas both sides till golden brown and crisp, turning over two to three times. This should take 6-7 minutes. Repeat the same procedure for the rest of the mix.

7. Take them out over paper towel, this absorb the access oil.

8. Serve vadas as they are or with chutneys. Taste best with coconut chutney (recipe ahead).

Aloo Chana Chaat

Recipe will serve 4.

Preparation time 30 minutes

Cooking time 10 minutes

Ingredients:

- 1-1/2 cups boiled chickpeas, garbanzo (chols, kabuli chana)
- 1-1/2 cups potatoes (aloo) boiled peeled and cubed in small pieces
- 1 tablespoon ginger finely grated (adrak)
- 2 teaspoons green chili finely chopped
- 1/4 teaspoon red chili powder
- 1 teaspoon roasted cumin seed powder
- 1/2 teaspoon salt
- 1/2 teaspoon black salt (kala namak)
- 1/2 teaspoon mango powder (amchoor)
- 2 teaspoons lemon juice
- 1/2 teaspoon sugar
- 2 tablespoons finely chopped cilantro (hara dhania)

For Garnishing

- 1 tomato finely chopped
- 6 slices of lemon
- 6 green chilies mild
- 2 tablespoons oil
- 1 teaspoon sea salt or coarse salt

Method

1. Wash and dry the whole green chilies. Heat a small frying pan on low medium heat, add the oil and green chilies, and cover the pan. Shake the pan slowly to move the chilies around. It is important to keep the pan covered, the chilies will splatter. Cook the chilies for about 2 minutes turn off the heat, wait till it stop splattering and remove the lid. Chilies should be light brown if it is not cook for another minute. Remove and keep aside.

2. Place chickpeas in a bowl and lightly mash. Add the potatoes and all the ingredients ginger, green chili, red pepper, salt, black salt, black pepper, mango powder, sugar, roasted cumin powder, lemon juice, and cilantro mix it well.

3. Let it sit for at least fifteen minutes or more, chickpeas and potatoes will absorbed the flavor of spices.

4. Serve the aloo chana chat with side of tomatoes, fried green peppers and lemon wedges.

How to boil the chickpea

Soak one cup of chickpeas for about eight hours or more, after soaking chick peas will be about 2-1/2 times. Drain the water, cooked the chickpeas in pressure cooker on high heat with 2 cups of water and no salt. After pressure cooker start steaming reduce the heat to low medium and cook for 10 minutes.

Jhaal Muri – Kolkata Puffed Rice Snack

This recipe will serve 4.

Ingredients:

- 4 cups murmura/ muri (puffed rice)
- 1/4 cup fine sev (bengal gram vermicelli)
- 1/4 cup peanuts
- 1 teaspoon oil
- 1/2 cup potato boiled, peeled and cut into small pieces
- 1/2 cup tomato finely chopped, seeded
- 1/2 cup cucumber finely chopped
- 2 tablespoons green chili, finely chopped, adjust to taste
- 2 tablespoons cilantro finely chopped (hara dhania)
- 1/4 cup tamarind paste
- 4 teaspoons mustard oil

Spice Mix

- 4 teaspoons roasted cumin seeds powder
- 1 teaspoon salt
- 1 teaspoon black salt
- 1 teaspoon mango powder (amchoor)
- 1 teaspoon red chili powder
- 1/2 teaspoon garam masala

4 slices of lemon for garnishing

Method

1. Combine all the dry spices together. Set aside.

2. Heat a 1 teaspoon of oil in a small pan on medium heat, add peanuts and roast stirring continuously till lightly brown. This should take about 2 minutes. Set aside.

3. Dry roast the muri/puffed rice on medium heat for about 3 minutes. Muri should not change color, they should be white but roasting gives freshness and makes them crispy. Set aside.

4. Just before serving jhaal muri add the peanuts, sev, tomato, potato, cucumber, green chili, cilantro, tamarind paste, mustard oil and spices. Toss them and serve.

5. You may adjust all the ingredients to your taste.

Aloo Chaat (Spicy Potato Snack)

This recipe will serve 4.

Preparation time 10 minutes

Cooking time 20 minutes

Ingredients:

- About 4 cups cubed potatoes, firmly boiled peeled and cut into bite size
- 3 tablespoons oil
- 1 teaspoon salt adjust to taste
- 1/4 cup cilantro finely chopped
- 1 tablespoon ginger thinly sliced
- 1 tablespoon green chili finely chopped, adjust to taste
- 2 teaspoons lemon juice

Spice Mix for Chaat Masala

- 1 tablespoon roasted cumin seed powder (bhuna jeera)
- 1 teaspoon red chili powder
- 1 teaspoon mango powder (amchoor)
- 1/4 teaspoon black pepper
- 1 teaspoons black salt
- 1/8 teaspoon asafetida
- 1/8 teaspoon citric acid
- 1/2 teaspoon ginger powder (saunth)
- 2 teaspoons sugar

Method

1. To make spice mix all the spice mix together really well and set aside.

2. Heat heavy flat frying pan on medium high heat, add the oil in to warm frying pan. Place the cubed potatoes on the frying pan and sprinkle the salt over the potatoes.

3. Stir fry the potatoes; turn them occasionally until all sides are golden brown. This process should take 8-10 minutes.

4. Turn off the heat and sprinkle ginger, cilantro, green chilies, lemon juice and about 1-1/2 tablespoons of spice mix. Mix it well, making sure all the pieces of potatoes are coated.

5. Taste one of the potato and add more spice mix if needed according to your taste.

Kulcha (Punjabi Flatbread)

Recipe will serve 2.

Ingredients:

- 1 cup of all purpose flour (plain flour or maida)
- 1/2 teaspoon baking powder
- 1/4 teaspoon baking soda
- 1/2 teaspoon salt
- 1/2 teaspoon sugar
- 1 tablespoon oil
- 2 tablespoon yogurt (curd or dahi)
- Approx. 1/4 cup milk use as needed

Also need

- 1/4 cup of all purpose flour for rolling
- 1/2 teaspoon nigella seeds (kalaunji)
- 1 tablespoon cilantro chopped (hara dhania)
- 1 tablespoon clarified butter, ghee

Method

1. In a bowl mix all the dry ingredients, flour, baking powder, baking soda, salt, and sugar, and sieve the flour to make sure even mixing.

2. Add oil and yogurt to the flour and mix it well, add milk as needed to make soft dough. Dough should be soft but not sticking to hand. Knead the dough to make smooth and pliable.

3. Cover the dough and let it sit for about 2 hours.

4. Knead the dough for few seconds and divide into four equal parts, roll them into patties. Take one patty press it in dry flour from both sides and roll in about 6" circle, if dough start sticking to the rolling pin or rolling surface dust little more dry flour.

5. Heat the skillet (iron skillet works the best) on medium heat. Skillet should be moderately hot. Wipe the skillet with few drops of oil.

6. Place the kulcha over skillet. Sprinkle few drops of water. Sprinkle few nigella seeds and little cilantro over the kulcha while kulcha is still wet, and press it with the spatula.

7. When the kulcha start to change color and start bubbling flip it over. There will be some golden brown spots. Wait about a minute and flip it over again.

8. Kulcha should have golden brown spots from both sides. Kulcha should not be cooked on high heat otherwise it will not cook through.

9. Kulcha is ready, butter the kulcha before serving.

Aloo Tikki (Potato Patties)

Makes 8 tikki.

Ingredients:

- 3 medium size potatoes boiled and shredded, to make 2 cups of shredded potato
- 2 tablespoon bread crumbs
- 1 teaspoon salt
- Oil for cooking

For the Filling

- 1/3 cup green peas boiled and drained
- 1 teaspoon chopped ginger
- 1 tablespoon green chili minced
- 1 tablespoon minced cilantro (hara dhania)
- ¼ teaspoon salt
- 1 teaspoon oil

For Serving

- About 1 cup yogurt whipped
- ¼ cup cilantro chutney
- ¼ cup tamarind chutney

Method

Making Filling

1. Boil and drain the water from the peas and lightly mash.

2. Heat the oil in a small pan over medium heat; add all the filling ingredients, stir fry for about two minutes. Keep the filling little moist. Set aside.

Making tikkis

1. Add the salt and bread crumb into the potatoes and knead to make the dough.

2. Divide the potatoes into 8 equal parts.

3. Takes one part of the potato dough, make a ball and flatten over the oiled palm. Put about 1 teaspoon of filling in the center and wrap around with potato. Lightly flatten the filled balls to patties. Make all the patties.

4. Heat non stick heavy skillet on medium high heat, generously greased the skillet. Place the tikkies on the skillet, making sure they are not touching each other and has some space all around. Oil the tikkies from the top.

5. Cook them for about 1 minute and turn them over, tikkies should be light golden brown. Oil the tikkies from the top and lightly press with spatula.

6. Turn the tikkies 3-4 times as needed to make sure tikkies are nice and crispy. Brush the oil lightly every time when you turn the tikkies over and also press with spatula.

7. Aloo tikkies taste best when they are served right from over the skillet.

8. You can prepare them in advance, up to five steps and brown them just before serving.

9. Tikkies are served along with tamarind chutney, cilantro chutney and yogurt. You can also serve them with spicy chole.

Dabeli Spicy Potato Sandwich

Serves 4

Ingredients:

Spice Mix

- 1 red chili dry
- 1 teaspoon coriander (dhania) seeds
- 2 cloves (laung / lavang)
- 1/2 inch cinnamon (dalchini)
- 1/2 teaspoon cumin (jeera) seeds
- 4 black pepper

Filling

- 1 cup potato boiled and mashed (aloo)
- 2 tablespoons oil
- 1/2 teaspoon cumin (jeera) seeds
- 1/2 teaspoon salt
- Spice mix which we prepared that should be about 1 tablespoon
- 1 tablespoon tamarind paste (imli)
- 3 teaspoons sugar
- 1/2 cup water

Also Need

- 4 buns
- 2 tablespoons butter for cooking

To Serve

- 1/4 cup roasted and crushed peanuts
- 1/4 cup fine sev available in Indian grocery stores

- 1/4 cup pomegranate (anar) seeds, if not available then grapes cut into small pieces
- 3 tablespoons cilantro chutney (dhania chutney)

Preparation

1. For Dabeli Masala: roast all the ingredients red chili, coriander, cloves, cumin seeds, cinnamon and black pepper, in a small pan on the medium heat for two minutes, spices will become very aromatic. Grind the spices to fine powder. This should make about one tablespoon.

2. For Filling: heat the oil in pan on medium heat moderately. Add cumin seeds when seeds crack add potatoes spice mix, salt and tamarind paste, mix it well.

3. Add about half cup of water mix it and bring to boil, cook on low heat for about two minutes. Mix should be consistency of thick paste. Set aside.

How to Proceed

1. Slice the buns into halves and toast the buns over skillet on medium heat using little butter both sides.

2. Over one half of the bun put about ¼ cup of the filling, top it with chutney, pomegranate, peanuts and fine sev (you can find in Indian grocery stores), sandwich with the other half of the bun.

Batata Vada – Aloo Bonda (Fried Potato Dumpling)

Serves 3

Ingredients:

- 3 medium potatoes boiled peeled and roughly chopped (2 cups of potatoes)
- 1 tablespoon oil
- 1/2 teaspoon black mustard seeds (rai)
- 7-10 curry leaves chopped, optional
- 1/4 teaspoon turmeric (haldi)
- 1 tablespoon finely chopped ginger
- 1 green chili finely chopped adjust to taste
- 2 tablespoons chopped cilantro (hara dhania)
- 1/2 teaspoon salt adjust to taste

For Batter

- 1/2 cup besan, gram flour (available in Indian grocery stores)
- 1 tablespoon rice flour
- 1/8 teaspoon asafoetida (hing)
- 1/4 teaspoon baking soda
- 1/4 teaspoon red pepper
- 1/2 teaspoon salt adjust to taste
- About 1/4 cup of water
- Oil to fry

Method

Batter

1. In a bowl mix besan, rice flour, salt, asafetida, pepper, and baking powder. Add water slowly to make a thick and smooth batter. Set aside.

Vada

1. Heat oil in a frying pan on medium heat moderately.

2. Add mustard seeds as the seeds crack add curry leaves, (curry leaves splatters) potatoes, ginger, green chili, turmeric, and salt.

3. Stir fry for about 3 minutes over medium heat. Add cilantro mix it well. Turn of the heat.

4. Let the potato mix cool off, divide them into about 12 pieces and make them into smooth round ball, they should be little smaller than golf balls.

5. Heat about 1"of oil in a frying pan on medium high heat. To check if the oil is ready, put one drop of batter in oil. The batter should come up but not change color right away.

6. Dip the potato balls into the batter one at a time, making sure the potato balls are completely covered with batter. Then, slowly drop them into the frying pan.

7. Turn them occasionally. Fry the batata vadas until all sides are golden-brown.

8. Batata vadas will take about four minutes to cook.

9. Serve them hot with cilantro chutney.

Kulfi (Indian Eggless Ice Cream)

This recipe will make 6-8

Ingredients:

- 4 cup milk
- 3/4 cup heavy cream
- 3/4 cup sugar
- 2 teaspoons corn starch
- 1/2 teaspoon agar-agar (sea weed works as a vegetarian gelatin)
- 1/4 teaspoon cardamoms crushed

Method

1. In a heavy bottom pan over medium high heat boil the milk, heavy cream, and sugar together.

2. After milk comes to boil lower the heat to medium and let it boil for about 35 minutes, stir the milk occasionally and clean the sides preventing milk not to make a ring on sides. Because of cream, milk does not burn in bottom of the pan.

3. In a small bowl mix corn starch, agar-agar, and cardamom with 2 spoons of water really well making sure there are no lumps,

4. Add to the boiling milk mix it well, boil for about 3 minutes. Turn off the heat and mix the milk for about a minute.

5. Let it cool and pour into the moulds, use Kulfi moulds, Popsicle moulds or small cups (approx 3 Oz).

6. Freeze for about 5 hours, before Kulfi is ready to serve.

Vegetable Frankie – Kathi Roll

This recipe will make 6 Frankies.

Ingredients:

For Roti

- 3/4 cup of all purpose flour
- 1/4 cup whole wheat flour
- 1/4 teaspoon salt
- 1 tablespoon oil
- Approx. 1/3 cup of water

Also Need

- 1/4 cup all purpose flour for rolling
- 1 tablespoon oil for brushing Frankies

For Filling

- 2 cups cabbage thinly sliced
- 1 cup carrot shredded
- 1/2 cup green peas
- 3/4 cup potatoes mashed
- 1/2 red bell pepper thinly sliced
- 1 cup tomato chopped
- 1 teaspoon finely shredded ginger
- 1 green chili finely chopped
- About 2 tablespoons cilantro chopped
- 2 tablespoons oil
- 1 teaspoon cumin seed
- 1 teaspoon salt

- 1/2 teaspoon garam masala

Method

For Filling

1. Heat the oil in sauce pan over medium high heat. Test the heat by adding one cumin seed to the oil; if the seed crack right away oil is ready.

2. Add cumin seeds as seeds crack add the ginger, cilantro and green chili, stir for few seconds.

3. Add tomatoes, and salt cook until tomatoes are tender this will take about 3-4 minutes.

4. Reduce the heat to medium and add cabbage, carrot, green peas, and bell pepper cook until vegetables are tender not mushy stir vegetables occasionally this should take 5-6 minutes.

5. Add potatoes to the vegetables mix it well. Turn off the heat and mix the garam masala.

6. Filling is ready. Set it aside.

For Roti

1. In a bowl mix whole wheat flour, all purpose flour, salt and oil. Add water to make firm and smooth dough, adjust the water as needed.

2. Knead the dough on a lightly oiled surface. Dough should not be sticking to the fingers.

3. Cover the dough and let it rest for about 10-15 minutes.

4. Knead the dough again and divide into 6 equal parts.

5. Take one part of the dough and press it both sides in dry flour this will help rolling. Roll it thin into about 9" diameter. If the dough sticks to the rolling pin or rolling surface, lightly sprinkle the dry flour.

6. Heat the skillet over medium high. Checks the skillet if it is hot enough. Sprinkle few drops of water over the skillet, water should sizzle. Skillet should not be smoking.

7. Place the roti over skillet for about half a minute, roti will change in the color lightly and puff different places.

8. Flip the roti over, and lightly press, flip it again roti should have light golden color on both sides.

9. Remove the roti from the skillet. Roti is ready. Make all the rotis, cover and set it aside.

Assembling the Frankie

1. Take one roti and put it over a flat surface. Put about ¼ cup of vegetable length wise leaving about 1-1/2 inch from the top and fold it tightly like burrito. Lightly brush the oil both sides of wrap.

2. Heat the skillet over medium heat. Place the Frankie over skillet and lightly brown both sides to nice and crispy.

3. Serve with Cilantro Chutney or Tamarind Chutney (recipe ahead).

CHUTNEYS

Hari Chutney – Cilantro Chutney

Ingredients:

- 1 big bunch of chopped Cilantro (green coriander)
- 3 green chopped chilies
- 3 tablespoons of lemon juice
- 1/2 inch ginger
- 1 1/2 teaspoon salt
- 1 teaspoon cumin seeds
- 1 teaspoon oil
- 1 teaspoon sugar
- Pinch of asafoetida (hing)

Method

1. Blend all ingredients, except the cilantro, into a paste. Add cilantro, a little at a time, and blend until smooth. Add water as needed.

2. Taste and adjust salt, green chilies, or lemon juice as desired.

Variations:

Mix mint leaves (without stems) with cilantro half and half.

Tamarind Chutney

Ingredients:

- 1/2 lb tamarind, seeded
- 2 1/2 cups sugar
- 2 cups boiling water
- 1 1/2 tablespoons roasted ground cumin seeds
- 1 tablespoon salt
- 1 teaspoon black salt
- 1 teaspoon red chili powder
- 1 teaspoon ground black pepper
- 1/2 teaspoon ginger powder

Method

1. Break the tamarind into small pieces and soak in boiling water for one hour.

2. Mash it into a pulp and strain, pressing the tamarind into the strainer to remove all the pulp. Add sugar to the pulp. Mix well. Add the remaining ingredients. Mix and taste. Add more sugar, salt or pepper as needed.

3. Chutney can be refrigerated for two to three months.

Coconut Chutney

Coconut chutney is a typical condiment that is served with South Indian dishes, especially Idlis and Dosas. It has great texture and a unique taste that compliments many dishes.

Serves 8.

Ingredients:

- 1 cup coconut peeled and cut in small pieces
- 2 tablespoon chana dal (available in Indian grocery stores)
- 1 cup of yogurt
- 1-1/2 teaspoons salt (adjust to taste)
- 2 Serrano green chilies cut in small pieces
- 1/2 inch ginger
- Approximately 1/2 cup water
- 1 teaspoon lemon juice (if needed)

For Seasoning

- 1 teaspoon oil
- pinch of asafetida
- 1/4 teaspoon black mustard seed
- 2 red chilies broken in pieces
- 6 to 8 curry leaves (1 sprig)

Method

1. Peel coconut and cut into small pieces for easy blending.

2. Roast chana dal on medium heat until it is light brown in color and has a roasted aroma.

3. Coarsely grind chana dal in a blender. Add yogurt, green chilies, and salt and continue blending into the paste.

4. Add coconut to the paste, a few pieces at a time and keep blending. Add water, as needed, to help with the grinding. (Adding the coconut in small amounts also helps this process).

5. Before removing from blender, taste chutney to adjust the salt and pepper. Use lemon juice to adjust the tang to suit your taste. Blend well.

Seasoning

1. Heat oil in small pan. When hot, add black mustard seeds.

2. When the seeds crack, add asafoetida, red chilies and curry leaves.

3. Pour the seasoning mixture over the chutney.

Coconut chutney can be refrigerated up to a week.

A Note of Thanks

"Towards the end, I really wish to thank you for downloading and reading this book. I genuinely hope you had as much fun trying out these recipes as I had putting them together for you.

Consider giving this book a positive review on Amazon Kindle.
I look forwards to your comments and feedback.

Thanks a Ton!
M. Fredrick